The Nature Kid's Guide to
CAMELS

DAVID ANDERSON

LP Media Inc. Publishing
Text copyright © 2026 by LP Media Inc.
All rights reserved.

For information address LP Media Inc. Publishing,
30012 Variolite St NW, Princeton MN 55371
www.lpmedia.org

Publication Data

Camels
The Nature Kid's Guide to Camels — First edition.

Summary: "Learn all about Camels, the Nature Kid Way"
— Provided by publisher.

ISBN: 979-8-89818-219-9

[1. Camels – Non-Fiction] I. Title.

Title: The Nature Kid's Guide to Camels

CONTENTS

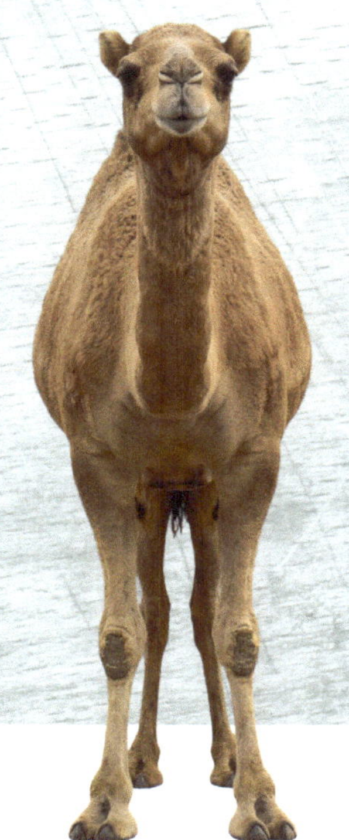

DESERT DWELLERS

Camels can gulp down 30 gallons of water in just 13 minutes — that's a whole bathtub!

Whoosh! A camel trots through a hot and sandy storm.

Imagine standing in a desert where the temperature hits 120 degrees and the nearest water is days away. Most animals would not last a week. Camels do not just survive — they thrive.

These incredible animals carry their own food supply on their backs, can gulp down a bathtub's worth of water in minutes, and crunch through plants covered in sharp spines without flinching. They have been outlasting every extreme the desert can throw at them for over 40 million years. There is no tougher animal alive.

CAMEL COUNTRY

Australia imported camels from Asia in the 1800s to explore the outback — when trucks replaced them, they were released and now live wild!

Crunch! A wild camel crosses the cold, rocky Gobi Desert.

There are two kinds of camel, and they could not look more different. The dromedary has one hump and lives in the hot deserts of Africa and the Middle East.

Wild Bactrian camels are very rare. They have two humps and roam the Gobi Desert in China and Mongolia. This desert is cold and rocky, not sandy at all. Winter temperatures can drop to minus 20 degrees!

Each species is perfectly built for its own home. Same family, very different worlds.

SUPER SIZED

A single camel hump can weigh
about 80 pounds — as much as
a second grader!

Thump! A huge camel stands tall on top of a desert dune.

A dromedary weighs up to 1,500 pounds and stands 7 feet tall at the hump — taller than most adults. The Bactrian camel is even bigger, with two humps and a thick shaggy coat built for freezing winters. Some Bactrians tip the scales at over 1,800 pounds.

Their size is one of their best defenses in the wild. Most predators think twice before approaching a fully grown camel. When size alone is not enough, camels can kick, bite, and spit — and they are not shy about using all three.

A camel has three eyelids on each eye — the third one is see-through and wipes away sand like a windshield wiper!

Poof! A camel shuts its nose tight as the wind blows.

Many people think camel humps are filled with water. They are not! The humps store fat, which the camel slowly burns for energy when food is hard to find. As the fat is used up, the hump shrinks and flops to one side.

Camels can also close their nostrils completely to block blowing sand. Thick curly lashes protect their eyes. Long legs keep them up off the scorching ground. Thick fur blocks the burning sun. Every part of a camel's body is a solution to a desert problem.

SANDY SENSES

Sniff! A camel lifts its head and smells water far away.

Camels have sharp senses built for desert life. Their big eyes can see far across the flat open landscape, spotting danger long before it gets close.

Their hearing is keen too. Camels pick up even soft sounds in the sand and swivel their ears toward any noise, always on alert.

A camel's nose may be the most impressive sense of all. It can sniff out water from surprisingly far away — a skill that can truly mean the difference between life and death in the scorching desert heat.

SPIT BACK

Watch out! An angry camel opens its mouth to say "get back"!

Camels have a gross way to fight back. When they feel upset, they spit. This spit is wet, green, and very stinky!

But this spit is not like your spit. It comes from deep in the belly and is mixed with stomach juices. It smells so bad that most animals run away fast.

Camels do not spit for fun. They only do it when scared or mad. It is their way of saying, 'Back off!' Most creatures only need one warning.

A camel's spit can fly through the air up to ten feet — and the smell can make you gag!

CACTUS CRUNCH

A camel can get enough water from the plants it eats to survive for two weeks without taking a single drink!

Munch! A camel bites into a prickly cactus and chews it up.

Camels eat plants that other animals skip. Thorny bushes and dry grasses make a fine meal. They even munch on cactus with sharp spines!

How do they do it? Their lips are thick and tough, almost like leather. Sharp thorns do not hurt them at all. A camel can crunch right through a prickly plant without flinching.

When water is hard to find, camels get moisture from the plants they eat. They also eat salty plants that grow near dry lakes. Nothing goes to waste in the desert.

CAMEL CALLS

FUN FACT!
A camel's bellow can be heard up to a mile away — that's about 20 football fields!

Groan! A camel lets out a long, loud rumble in the sand.

Camels are not quiet animals. They groan, moan, and **bellow**. Some calls are soft whispers. Others are loud enough to hear from far away.

A mother camel hums gently to her calf. The baby calls back with a soft cry. These sounds help them find each other in a crowded **herd**.

When a camel is upset, it lets out a long, deep roar. It may also grumble or snort. Each sound means something different, and other camels understand every one.

WATCH OUT
20

Growl! A wolf pack creeps closer to a herd of wild camels.

Wild camels face real dangers. Wolves are their biggest **predators**. A hungry pack may try to chase a young or weak camel for hours.

Wolves hunt best in winter. Snow makes it hard for camels to run fast. Baby calves are the ones most in danger during these cold months.

But grown camels are very hard to take down. Their huge size keeps most hunters away. Being part of a herd makes them even harder to attack.

Long ago, wild camels also had to watch out for desert lions and saber-toothed cats!

KICK HARD

A camel can kick forward, backward, and even sideways — predators never know what's coming!

Wham! A camel sends a powerful kick with its back leg.

Camels are not easy to bother. When a predator gets too close, a camel may kick with its strong back legs. One powerful kick can send a wolf flying through the air.

Camels can also bite if they need to. Their big teeth and strong jaws make a crushing bite. Most animals learn quickly to keep away.

Running is another great escape. A camel can sprint up to 40 miles per hour in short bursts! That is fast enough to outrun most danger in the desert.

SAND STRUT

DID YOU KNOW?
A camel's foot pad spreads as wide as a dinner plate when it steps down!

Stomp! A camel's wide feet press into the soft, warm desert sand.

Camels walk in a special way. Both legs on the same side move at once. This gives them a smooth, swaying walk — like a boat rocking on gentle waves.

Their wide, flat feet help them walk on sand without sinking. The soft pads spread out with each step. It is like wearing big snowshoes!

Camels walk slowly most of the time to save energy for long trips. But when they need to move fast, they can really run. A camel can travel 25 miles in a single day.

DAY DRIFTERS

26

Chomp! A camel chews a wad of food for the second time today.

Camels have a quiet daily life. They spend most of the day walking and eating. When the sun is hottest, they rest in the shade or lie down together.

Camels chew their food twice. They swallow it, then bring it back up and chew it again. This is called chewing **cud**. It helps them get every bit of nutrition from tough desert plants.

At night, camels lie down on the sand. They tuck their legs under their bodies to stay warm. The cool night air helps them rest after a long, hot day.

CARAVAN CREW
FUN FACT!
Female camels often stay in the same herd for their whole lives!

Thump! A line of camels marches across the sandy dune together.

Camels are social animals. They live in groups called herds. A herd can have up to 30 camels or more traveling together.

One strong male leads the group. The females and their young stay close together in the middle. They feel safer surrounded by the herd.

Camels look out for each other. If one senses danger, it warns the rest with a loud call. Together, they are much stronger than they would be alone.

FINDING LOVE

A mating contest between two male camels can last over an hour — and get very slobbery!

Gurgle! A male camel puffs out a big, pink blob from its mouth.

Male dromedary camels put on one of the wildest shows in the animal kingdom to win a mate. They push a soft, pink pouch called a **dulla** out of their mouths — it looks like a floppy balloon! They gurgle, drool, and foam while puffing up to look as impressive as possible.

If two males want the same female, they shove and wrestle until one gives up. This competition happens once a year during mating season. The strongest male wins. The rest walk off and wait for next year.

CUTE CALVES

Baby camels are born without a hump — it grows as they start eating solid food!

Plop! A newborn camel calf tumbles onto the warm desert sand.

A camel mom has one baby at a time. The calf grows inside her for about 13 months. That is longer than a human baby!

A newborn calf can stand within just a few hours. Its long legs are wobbly at first. But soon, it can walk right next to its mom.

Baby camels are born with soft, fluffy fur. They can see and hear right away. Within a day, the little calf trots along with the herd, ready to explore the desert.

GOOD MOMS

DID YOU KNOW?
A mother camel can pick out her own calf by smell alone — even in a herd of hundreds!

Hum! A mother camel nudges her calf gently with her warm nose.

Mother camels take great care of their young. A mom will nurse her calf for up to a year or even longer. She stays near it at all times.

Bactrian camel moms are especially caring. They lick and nuzzle their babies often. They teach the calf how to find food and water in the harsh desert.

If danger comes near, the mother steps in front of her baby. She stands tall and will not move an inch. A camel mom is one of the bravest animals in the desert.

TOUGH TIMES

DID YOU KNOW?
The Wild Bactrian camel is rarer than the giant panda — there are only about 950 left!

Crack! The dry ground splits under the hot sun once again.

Life is getting harder for wild camels. The Wild Bactrian camel is one of the rarest big animals on Earth. Fewer than 1,000 are left in the wild today.

Droughts dry up the water they need. People build on the land where they live. Some camels are hunted, too.

These problems make life harder every year. Without help, wild camels could disappear forever. We must act now to keep these amazing animals safe.

HELP HERDS

The Great Gobi Reserve in Mongolia is one of the largest protected areas on Earth!

Click! A ranger takes a photo of a rare wild camel on a rocky hill.

People around the world are working hard to protect wild Bactrian camels.

Scientists travel deep into the Gobi Desert to study these rare animals up close. They attach small GPS trackers to camels and follow where the herds go. This helps them figure out which water sources the camels need most and which land must be kept safe.

It is careful, patient work — but it is giving wild camels a better chance at survival.

GLOSSARY

herd

A group of animals that live and travel together

dulla

A soft pink pouch that male camels push out of their mouths to impress a mate

bellow

A loud, deep call or cry

cud

Food that comes back up to be chewed a second time

predator

An animal that hunts and eats other animals

9 798898 182199